Sheffield Hallam University Press
Learning Centre
City Campus
Pond Street
Sheffield S1 1WB

Designed by Design Studio, Learning Centre, Sheffield Hallam University

All rights reserved. No part of this publication may be
reproduced, stored in a retrieval system, or transmitted
in any form or by any means, electronic, mechanical,
photocopying, recording, or otherwise, without prior
written permission of the publishers.

©1998   ISBN 0 86339 810 3

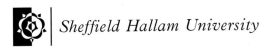

Dedication
'To Roy for all his patience and encouragement'

Yorkshire Craftsmen at Work

A Unique Photographic Survey of a Living Tradition by
David Morgan Rees

David Morgan Rees, who lives in Ilkley, worked in industry until 1985 before he became a part-time academic, lecturing in PR Studies at the University of Leeds, Leeds Business School and other establishments. As a freelance writer and photographer, he now concentrates on rural subjects and over many years has contributed to BBC Radio and publications like 'Yorkshire Life', The Dalesman' and Yorkshire Journal'.

First Published 1981
Revised Edition 1998

'Yorkshire has never been purely agricultural. There was iron and steel smelting from earliest times. There was ship-building and important fishing, a prosperous whaling industry; and the county long had the monopoly of the alum trade. Whitby jet carvers, Yorkshire craftsmen in gold, Ripon spur makers, and elsewhere clock makers, saddlers, ham and bacon curers all gained eminence. Metal was won from Yorkshire ores in primitive charcoal-heated furnaces in the Middle Ages. All these varied industries have given the county a heritage, which has been built up from the time when Yorkshire was the home of several monastic Orders, all of which by their skill laid the foundation of the County's greatness.'

J & R Fairfax-Blakeborough: The Spirit of Yorkshire (Batsford 1954).

Front Cover: Wilf Hutchinson, a furniture maker at Husthwaite, near Coxwold, was apprenticed to Robert Thompson, the 'Mouse Man' of Kilburn, and follows in a long and distinguished tradition of fine furniture-making in Yorkshire.

Back Cover: Top - Left: Bob Guy cutting a stone roof slate to size;
Right: Fred Bently, maker of shepherd's crooks.
Centre - Left: Margery Stones, Wensleydale Cheese-maker
Right: Geoff Lund, Dales Waller.
Bottom Left: John Harding, champion gatemaker of Kirkby Misperton;
Right: Billy Clarkson, Whitby coble-builder.

Contents

	Page
Preface	i
Introduction	1
Stone North York Moors Stone Mason • Dales Village Vernacular Building • Dry Stone Walling • Millwright	8
Wood Wheels, Carts and Wagons • Farm Implements • Besoms • Country Furniture Maker • Walking Sticks and Shepherds' Crooks • The Cooper • Clogging • Coble Builder	16
Wool Handloom Weavers • Teazling • Shuttle Making • Tailor	40
Clay The Potter	48
Straw, Willow and Fibre Crab Pots •Thatcher • Basket Maker • Ropes and Nets • Corn Dollies	50
Metal Blacksmith and Farrier • Dales Tinsmith	58
Leather Saddlers • Village Bootmaker	64
The 'Little Mesters' of Sheffield Knife blade • Forger • Grinder • Penknife Cutler • Silversmith • Horn Cutters • Mother of Pearl	68
Ecclesiastical Crafts Master Mason • Glazier • Clockmakers	78
Domestic and Decorative Knitting • Rug prodding • Lace • Quilting • Farmhouse Cheese • Staithes bonnets • Jet Carving	83
Sport and Leisure Cricket Bats • Brass Band Instruments	92

Preface

CRAFTSMANSHIP - the skill of making things by hand, of practical use rather than for pure decoration - is a deeply personal and intuitive activity which often defies the rational approach of engineer or industrial designer. In a craftsman's work the end result depends on the decisions made as the work develops whereas in a machine-made article, shape, colour and texture are all determined before production begins. Traditional craftsmen are united by an intense concern for the job in hand because they see it through from the raw material to the finished object. Their obvious personal satisfaction is enviable.

Craftsmen are the 'survivors', struggling with patience and modesty against the developing patterns of society and yet always seeming to adapt to the standards of their customers, managing to stand outside the cycles of technological and commercial change although affected by these, with their work providing a touchstone of older, more formal values.

These photographs of Yorkshire craftsmen - and women - in town and country were taken during the 'seventies. Sadly, some of the individuals have died since I photographed them at work and others have retired. But this book remains, I hope, a unique and comprehensive visual record of these talented and resourceful people whom I was privileged to meet.

Happily the future of my photographs is now secure as an archive held as the David Morgan Rees Collection at the Psalter Lane Campus Library, part of the Library and Learning Resources of Sheffield Hallam University. A selection of the photographs has been exhibited under the title 'Privileged People' in a number of centres in Yorkshire.

I acknowledge the inspiration I have received from the work of Marie Hartley and Joan Ingilby whose remarkable texts and photographs of life and tradition in Yorkshire in their many publications have been a fascinating source of knowledge and interest for me. I would also like to thank John Kirby and Richard Swift of the Psalter Lane Library and Monica Moseley of Sheffield Hallam University Press for their encouragement, support and tireless attention to detail.

David Morgan Rees

Introduction

An Historical Background to Yorkshire Crafts

Yorkshire's sheer size has helped to keep many of its traditional crafts alive. Inevitably tenuous early communications between people in dale, moorland or wold communities, emphasised their isolation and the consequent need for self-sufficiency in providing such essentials as clothing, furniture and utensils as well as tools to gain a living from the land. There are still one or two areas today where pockets of rural craftsmanship seem unaffected by contemporary influence.

Yorkshire also provides a graphic illustration of the importance of country and town on craftsmen, of how in medieval times crafts have moved from early town centres like York, Beverley or Pontefract where guilds were strong, monopolistic and inflexible to country areas where yeoman farmers used their skills and initiative and then back again to other urban areas in the late eighteenth century as the Industrial Revolution gathered momentum. The woollen trade followed this pattern, bringing with it such ancillary activities as blacksmithing, foundry work and shuttle-making. Later Sheffield's cutlery trade showed a somewhat similar movement, from pleasant outlying country districts where water power was freely available towards the grimness of the growing city centre, to meet the voracious demand of the big cutlery firms in the Victorian age for the handiwork of cutlers which was despatched all over the world.

Although traces of the primitive craftsmanship of Yorkshire's early inhabitants and settlers, whether of ornament or weaponry, have been found in lonely Celtic burial mounds or in Roman encampments, it was still not until after the Norman Conquest, under the influence of the ideas and trade, art and learning which passed between Normandy and England, that there was any real flowering of craftsmanship in Yorkshire and other Northern areas. The great expressions of creativity like York, Ripon and Beverley Minsters are essentially of Norman inspiration as are many of Yorkshire's village churches.

In the twelfth century that remarkable religious order, the Cistercians, had a profound influence on medieval craftsmanship, in the building of their great abbeys of Fountains, Rievaulx and Jervaulx. As well as being industrious farmers, cheese-makers and quarrymen, they were skilled craftsmen themselves, gathering about them many talented lay workers, such as stone-.

masons and smiths. They were the chief shepherds in Yorkshire at this time, founding its woollen trade with the assistance of Flemish weavers who settled here in the twelfth and thirteenth centuries.

Another key feature of medieval craft activity was the craft and merchant guilds. No man could follow his craft calling or trade unless he was a member of such a guild. It was as dominant as any modern trade union. It enabled men to keep an eye on each other's activity by ensuring that those who followed a similar craft had their workshops as close together as possible. Thus such streets as Ropergate in Pontefract or the Shambles in York are evidence of ropemakers or butchers. The glaziers and glass-painters tended to gather together in Stonegate in York. York itself had up to 60 guilds while Pontefract had 38 at the height of their power and activity.

At the same time Doncaster, Selby, Wakefield, Sheffield and Bradford also grew in importance, each with a nucleus of craftsmen supplying a developing urban community. Similar craftsmen were also in evidence in the larger villages. Blacksmith, joiner, wheelwright, tinker, potter and millwright offered their skills not only in service to their feudal lord but also by barter between their equals in the village.

In the ordered feudal society, at its height in the thirteenth century, each craftsman knew his rights and his duties. His rights extended, besides his dwelling, to a small enclosure, a few strips in the open fields at the edge of the village and grazing on common land on fell or moor. The craftsman provided goods for his lord in lieu of the labour expected of the other villagers. However, the Black Death which came to Yorkshire in 1349 altered the shape and functioning of that society with its decimation of human life. The lord could no longer exploit the craftsman. Work was now a cash transaction. The Wars of the Roses were a further disruption, leaving the nobility in the North weakened and humbled. By the end of the fourteenth century the regime of the feudal manor had largely been destroyed and the lord became more of a commercial landlord to his tenants.

The sixteenth century Dissolution of the Monasteries left the great abbeys of Yorkshire stripped bare of their treasures and roofless, dispersing all those craftsmen whose lives had been so closely bound up with the religious orders. The skill and experience of those stone masons who worked on the abbeys and monasteries were now employed elsewhere on churches, bridges, houses and a variety of other stone buildings.

By the end of the Middle Ages craft work was no longer confined to isolated rural areas or to the tightly-knit guilds. With the development of a more advanced village economy, with the ending of feudalism, many village trades had widened their scope and in so doing had become mutually dependent. For example, cartwrights, wheelwrights, blacksmiths and harness-makers had a clear community of interests and worked increasingly closely together. At seaports boat builders were dependent in turn on sail and rope-makers. Coopers, too, and tackle-makers would have had their part to play. There were also developments in mining, whether of iron-stone, lead or coal, iron-smelting and quarrying following the pioneering work of the ubiquitous Cistercians.

The maturing sixteenth-century was the age both of the Reformation and the Renaissance in Tudor England. Inevitably this affected a number of institutions and traditions which had been created in the Middle Ages. The craft guilds in the towns at the height of their effectiveness in the thirteenth and fourteenth centuries, could not now adapt to the new pressures for change and expansion. At their best the guilds ensured the training of apprentices, a high standard of work, honesty of dealing, and the provision of a considerable welfare care for members and their families. But the strength of these institutions became their weakness. An entrenched paternalism, with a monopolistic, closed-shop attitude stifled creativity and caused wide-spread frustration. This inflexibility was quickly countered by the new capitalist merchanting system. All effective power began to pass from the collective guilds to the emergent distributive trades. The domestic 'cottage' system of craftsmanship in village and hamlet showed a greater adaptability and enterprise than the prestigious but ponderous guilds.

Nowhere is this better seen than in Yorkshire's wool trade. The important trade in wool and wool textile exports, traditionally the profitable concern of York, declined as the Tudor age developed. It was killed off by guild regulations which insisted on limiting the number of apprentices available to craftsmen, demanding a rigid demarcation between tailors, glovers, drapers and mercers and laying down fixed measurements and methods of working. Coverlet workers, for example, were restricted to working on a single loom with even the types of yarn being prescribed. The River Ouse at York became increasingly difficult to navigate and so Hull took on the role of merchanting and export centre. As York declined so did Beverley, but their loss became the gain of the West Riding. Increasingly wool workers such as 'speynners, carders and other necessary work-folkes' were seen in the streets of the growing towns of Halifax, Leeds, Bradford and Wakefield. It was said in Henry VIII's reign that Wakefield 'standith all by clothing.'

With the transformation of the Tudor business scene in Yorkshire a new middle class developed from an increasingly prosperous yeoman stock. They were a peaceful influence, so different from an earlier nobility who lived defensively in such homes as Nappa Hall in Wensleydale with its pele tower or moated Markenfield Hall near Ripon. This new found wealth was spent on the building of the spectacular designs of Burton Agnes and Burton Constable or the splendour of Temple Newsam House near Leeds. These new capitalists actively encouraged both artist and craftsmen.

These broadened horizons were suddenly restricted in the mid-seventeenth century by the Civil War with the influence of Cromwell and his followers. The Puritan avoidance of frivolity and ornamentation had a curious effect upon the work of certain craftsmen. Furniture makers, for example, previously commissioned to produce fashionably elaborate designs, reverted to simpler styles which were traditionally native to the area. There was now a great depression in the wool textile trade.

The West Riding clothing towns were badly affected and exports of cloth declined to a low level. The Restoration was especially welcome in this part of Yorkshire because it was seen as relief for 'the particular Decay and Ruine of the Clothing Trade of this County.' A measure to stimulate the trade was Charles II's decree that every corpse should be buried in a woollen shroud.

The North, which had been so raided and fought over, drifted into a more peaceful era with the political spotlight firmly on London. Men in commerce now commissioned sturdy dwellings of substance but not flamboyance like Shibden Hall, Halifax, Bolling Hall, Bradford, and East Riddlesden Hall, Keighley.

In the seventeenth century there was still no clear differentiation between craft and industry. Both relied on skill and manual dexterity. Craft activity required a few hands to produce a finished article or complete a process whereas industry was an alliance of mutually dependent skills. The tanning of leather is an example of an activity where craft skills were part of an emergent industrial trade. But as the country's economy developed, with the dawning of the eighteenth century, demand began to outstrip supply, exceeding all the efforts of individual craftsmen to meet it. Manufacturing industry stepped in to satisfy new levels of demand. Although the eighteenth century represented the highest peak of English craftsmanship, inevitably a gulf began to develop between the village craftsman and the factory worker. In 1724 Daniel Defoe in his Tour through the 'Whole Island of Great Britain' presented the West Riding as having 'the greatest share of wealth, as it has also of people'. Halifax was 'not to be equalled in England' as a commercial centre while Leeds, in his eyes, was 'a noble scene of industry and application'. Doncaster was a 'noble, large and spacious town, exceeding populous, and a great manufacturing town, principally for knitting.'

Defoe in his enthusiasm may have overplayed the extent of industrial activity so early in the century, but undoubtedly Yorkshire was soon to witness the gathering pace of the Industrial Revolution as many hand processes were taken over by machines. This was particularly the case in the wool textile industry, which for so long had been a 'cottage' activity in rural areas. Inventions like Hargreaves' Spinning Jenny in 1766, Arkwright's water-driven spinning frame and Cartwright's steam-powered loom in 1789 were soon to cause a complete transformation of industry and, inevitably, a number of traditional craft skills in Yorkshire.

By the mid-eighteenth century Sheffield's cutlery craftsmen, the 'little mesters' (as the men who combined running a small farm with their craft were called), had begun to benefit from the invention of crucible steel by Benjamin Huntsman. As well as aiding the growth of Sheffield's steel industry, steam power was also to provide the cutlery trade with power for a greater output and variety of edge tools for which the city became famous in the nineteenth century with a flourishing export trade to many corners of the world.

Steam power also had a pervasive effect upon the pattern of country crafts. There was a considerable exodus of country people to the new towns where factory owners were hungry for labour. The small rural home industries like the Wensleydale knitting of mittens and stockings could no longer compete with factory-made articles. Another influence was the opening up of the Yorkshire countryside by improved communications. Villages became more accessible, emerging from their traditional isolation. It was only in 1759, for example, that a road was made across the North Yorks Moors, from Pickering to Whitby. Before that, travellers used the old horse 'wynds', a series of stone slabs laid through the heather. At the same time villages were exposed to outside sources of supply for goods and services which had hitherto been the exclusive province of local craftsmen and traders. These new items brought by travelling salesmen were mostly factory-made, with novelty value but lacking the quality and dependability of the craftsman's handiwork.

From 1850 to 1870 agriculture flourished with a consequent opening for many rural industries, some of which later became industrial giants, like Fowler of Leeds, originally a maker of ploughs and other agricultural implements. This prosperity was only brought to an end by the terrible summer of 1879, noted at that time as being the wettest on record. From then on British agriculture ceased to be the sole supplier of the nation's food. The old rural order began to break up as did the traditions of country craftsmanship. Victorian industry was dependent on cheap exports, needing cheap imports of raw material and cheaper methods of working. Manufacturers needed more and more 'hands' for their mills and factories and so the exodus from the country to the town increased. Additionally many other small traditional country industries such as tanning, milling, brewing and ironfounding moved nearer their main markets and sources of raw materials in the larger towns. Crafts like tailoring and bootmaking also became more of an urban activity.

Although Leeds' wealth was based since the early seventeenth century on wool and textiles there were many other activities in engineering and manufacturing which brought the city renown. Like Sheffield with its sub-structure of skills carried out by the 'little mesters', Leeds also had a wide variety of crafts which were followed, often in appalling conditions, in workshops above and behind its busy streets. These town crafts are sometimes not as easy to identify as those of the country. They ranged from goldsmiths to bellfounders to barrel-organ makers to the distinctive Leedsware pottery, now as sought after by collectors as the work of the Rockingham potteries near Doncaster. They illustrate the brief moment in the Victorian age when traditional urban craftsmanship partnered or served industrial manufacture and was carried out by men whose skill was well acknowledged.

Two world wars in the twentieth century had their effect upon crafts in town and country. These major disruptions accelerated the pace of change in Yorkshire as elsewhere in the country despite small, defiant pockets of resistance. The sweeping advances by the plastics industry in the fifties and sixties made inroads into the work of potters, tinsmiths, woodturners, joiners and furniture makers. Imports of craft goods from the third world have had a significant effect, too. both in diverting business away from local craftsmen and yet in stimulating a new interest in handicrafts, from which they in turn are now beginning to benefit.

Some crafts have survived in Yorkshire more robustly than others. There has been considerable contraction in their numbers but extinction is not imminent. The Rural Development Commission is playing a vital part in helping craftsmen to learn new methods as well as encouraging young men to get a sound basic training with many types of craft courses, from blacksmithing to thatching to saddlery.

Perhaps Yorkshire is lucky, once again, because of its size. There is a greater chance that distance between the rural areas of the Dales, the North Yorks Moor, the Wolds and the towns will preserve the individuality of village life, its values and remaining craft traditions than in some of the more crowded areas further south. But it is sad to think that there may have been other crafts which could perhaps have been saved if only their contemporary function could have been identified and resources devoted to develop them to a new significance and usefulness while there was still time to preserve traditions and skills.

Stone

North York Moors Stone Mason

Robert Weatherill, monumental and general stone mason, at work on a piece of freestone in his yard at Danby, Eskdale, in the Cleveland Hills.

You only have to listen for a short time to a stone mason talking about his craft and the material he uses to realise that stone can be almost as individual and tricky as wood to work with. Most stone masons seem to have had experience of cutting stone in a quarry as well as patiently, lovingly fashioning it into a whole building or a fireplace or into a gravestone to stand in a country churchyard. So they know how stone will match up to its end use, how it will carve and how it will weather. As well as the variations of character and durability between, say, limestone, gritstone or sandstone, a particular type of stone will vary from one quarry to another in the same area. This is the case with the variety of sandstone known as 'freestone' because of its easy working quality. It is found widely in the North York Moors area and is used in many of the farmhouses, cottages and churches.

In the days before the large quarrying companies, most of the stone was worked by families of stone masons who had access to small quarries within reasonable distance of the project for which the material was needed. They paid the local landlord an agreed rate for whatever stone was removed from the quarry. Often if you look in the vicinity of a farmhouse or barn you will see the source of the stone used in its building in the remains of a small quarry.

Robert Weatherill, at Shaw End quarry above Great Fryupdale where several generations of his family have quarried their stone.

The principal tools of the stone mason's trade.

The craftsmanship of another generation of monumental masons in St Hilda's churchyard, Danby.

Dales Village Vernacular Building

Yorkshire Dales villages have a solidarity and a visual unity - qualities which were first created by village craftsmen, whether stone mason or joiner, in a long line of tradition which began with the 'cruck' building around the 14th century. This was the first time that a building was more than just a shelter from the elements for country people. During the 16th and 17th centuries these simple homes were rebuilt from locally quarried stone to accommodate both growing families and stock as farms prospered. At the same time bays were added which provided the familiar form of the 'long house' seen in the upper Dales which has lasted with few variations until today.

One of the finest examples in the tradition of Dales vernacular building, the 17th century West New House in Bishopdale where the farmhouse and barn are all under one roof.

The line of tradition with its strong imprint on architectural style has been dictated as much by the materials which were available locally in days when slender communications prevented the arrival of many distracting influences from the outside world as by the sturdy workmanship of the men who built these villages and farm buildings, the stone masons who were content to repeat their simple methods in traditional materials because they knew they were good and proof against the savagery of the Northern elements.

A Swaledale cottage is re-roofed in the traditional way with stone slates.

These traditions continue amongst the craftsmen who build today in the Dales. Many a small firm of Dales building contractors is still able to employ craftsmen who come from families who possess a remarkable continuity of skill and experience.

Bob Guy of the Reeth builders, Blenkiron & Co. using a slater's hammer to cut a stone roof slate to size.

The old method of fixing roof slates was with wood pegs. Today alloy nails are used.

11

Dry Stone Walling

Geoff Lund, a Dales waller, at work on the foundation for a limestone wall on Wassa Hill above Conistone in Wharfedale.

Dry stone walling is one of the toughest and most basic of country crafts. Handed down from father to son, the skill and hard work have preserved a dominant feature of the Yorkshire Dales landscape. The lines etched firmly on slopes and fells are as typical and unmistakably of the Dales as the small, neat shippons built to shelter beast or fodder.

In the Middle Ages walls were built to establish boundaries between the land of one village and the next rather than to prevent cattle and sheep straying. It was only in the 16th century, as the wool trade flourished and so a better grade of sheep was reared that more care was given to their grazing. With a growing need to improve pasture, parts of the outlying common land or 'waste' on the moors were enclosed with stone walls for the first time. At the same time villagers were allowed by landowners to enclose small 'crofts' of ground next to their homes for the growing of special crops for domestic or animal use.

In the 18th century the demand grew from larger and more powerful landowners to enclose wider areas of land with new methods of agriculture needing more land. The villager with his age-old rights of common grazing was a nuisance. A series of private Acts of Parliament was promoted to give landowners the right to enclose this land. Much of the walling seen on the higher slopes of the Dales is directly as a result of separating the villager from his

rights to use the common land freely.

Thus the walls in the Dales are an intriguing witness to important and unfortunate pressures in the past. Today they are a help, rather than a deprivation for the average Dales farmer, despite the considerable amount of hard work involved in their upkeep.

The hammer is the waller's only tool for breaking and shaping the stone to suit his needs.

Geoff Lund, a waller since leaving school, places a topstone to finish a section of wall.

Millwright

The local water mill was once a focal point of village life, fulfilling a vital role in the whole inter-locking economy of the area it served. The products which it produced from the harvested grain went to feed man and beast. It was part of the slow-turning cycle of rural life. The discontinuity affecting the age-old balance of agriculture caused by its closure in all but a few places in Britain was more far-reaching than one might at first imagine.

Long days and hard work- that was the pattern of the miller's life as wagons brought grain from the surrounding countryside and took out the finished article of flour, 'sharps', bran and other feeding stuff for animals. A significant feature was the efficiency of the whole production cycle. Nothing was wasted.

When there was not flour and meal to be delivered, there was plenty of maintenance work to do. An important part of this was the dressing of the mill-stones by a millwright or by the small millowner himself. There was a need to dress them three or four times during the winter depending upon the grain being milled. The type of dress had to suit the type of grain being ground. If the weather was damp and the air humid, the mill stones could clog up and so there

Arthur Robinson was the fourth generation of a family who operated Rievaulx Mill (opposite) for 150 years until it closed down in 1961. As well as milling and delivering the flour he regularly maintained the mill-stones by 'dressing' them in the tradition of millwrighting.

was a need to clean them out from time to time. Usually the dressing was done in the evenings by candle-light because there was no time during the day when the mill was at its busiest.

Wood

Wheels, Carts and Wagons

Today horse drawn wagons and carts are either museum pieces or the devoted pastime of a minority of enthusiasts but in the hey-day of their past in the country before the tractor displaced the horse as surely as the horse had displaced the ox, these farm vehicles were hard-working examples of functional design in which the rural craftsman's skill and natural sense of shape and form were possibly at their most developed.

Though variations of type and style can be seen in different parts of the country, generations of knowledge and custom evolved a basic design that worked with simplicity and was capable of continual repair and renewal as one part wore out. The parts were made exactly to suit their chosen purpose without the aid of plans of drawings but with an innate sense of what worked. The shafts were shaped and balanced to suit the horse. The wheels themselves were designed and made to run with the maximum weight to be carried in the cart over a variety of terrain in all weathers.

Three generations of the Sissons family hooping wheels at Beswick, near Driffield - Percy, his son Cyril and grandson Bernard.

In the larger villages in the more prosperous areas farm wagons and carts were built by teams of craftsmen. Carpenters made the body and the underframe, the wheelwright the wheels, the blacksmith the metal tyres or strakes for the wheels, and the painter decking out the finished vehicle in its glory of colour. But in many of the small Yorkshire villages it was more likely to be the village carpenter who would build the body and make the wheels himself as well as being farm implement and coffin maker and undertaker.

Cyril Sissons, son of Percy Sissons, with a demonstration model to show how a wagon wheel is constructed, with central 'naff' or hub of elm, spokes of oak and felloes of ash.

Lifting the heated hoop or tyre from the fire.

Hammering the wooden wheel into its heated metal tyre on the hooping plate.

Water prevents the wood burning while the metal tyre contracts to the right fit.

18

Three generations of craftsmen with their handiwork.

Percy Sissons, in his eighties, man of many wheels - and wagons.

A corner of the Sissons yard, at Beswick, near Driffield.

An East Yorkshire farm wagon made by the Sissons family at Beswick around 1890.

Farm Implements - Hayrake and gate

Ronnie Haygarth with a hayrake made at his home in Dent.

O ne of the great delights in examining the work of craftsmen is the fact that more often than not the objects they make have an inherent grace and integrity as well as practicality. They are as good to look at as to handle. The hayrakes made by Ronnie Haygarth of Dent are a fine example. Lovingly and patiently made from wood throughout, without a single nail or dab of glue, they are simple objects that would ornament a room as much as help a farmer gather in his hay crop. What is more they are still in great demand by Dales farmers who continue to use them as their fore-fathers did in the crannies of small steep meadows where no tractor can work safely. After he retired from active work as a joiner in the village of Dent (now in Cumbria), he continued to make a hayrake of a style and strength belonging to a long rural tradition.

A well-made wooden gate kept in good working order on a farm is a most satisfying sight, but, alas, rather a rare one these days. Many farmers spend little time and money on their gates and fences, preferring to resort to compromise with all manner of extraordinary ways of patching them up and prolonging their life with relics of bedsteads, wire-netting, barbed wire and baler twine. Sometimes farm gates resemble some crazy kind of sculpture rather than what is essentially an important means of enabling the farmer to work efficiently on his land. It seems a surprising piece of short-sightedness on the farmer's part. A well-made gate in good quality timber, although more expensive than a cheaper version, and kept in good order, is ultimately an economy and capable of saving time and temper. A metal gate, however practical and strong, simply does not have the character and grace of something stoutly made by a craftsman.

John Harding, champion gatemaker and winner of many prizes at Yorkshire shows, at Kirkby Misperton, near Pickering.

Besoms

Fred Hall, of Pickering, prepares the 'ling' or heather to form the head of a besom.

The besom is a simple example of the craftsman's resourcefulness in making the best use of available raw materials. The besom itself is a very functional object for sweeping, particularly lawns and paths. In other parts of the country it was made from specially gathered birchwood which was stored and dried during the winter. But in Yorkshire, the North Yorkshire Moors, in particular, provided an ample source of effective material in the form of ling (or heather) which was there for easy gathering and for making instantly into besoms without the need for winter-long storage.

Besom-making provided a pitifully modest living for many people in the area. Besoms were used on the farms and in factories, and until the last war there was a constant demand. It is only since the introduction of modern, mass-produced cleaning materials, like brushes with plastic bristles and the proliferation of detergents and other cleansing agents that something as simple and cheap as a besom has fallen from favour, although there are still many gardeners of the old school who swear that there is nothing as efficient as a besom for sweeping a path or a lawn.

Using the 'knippers' to compress the ling.

Binding the besom head using a strip of ash as 'wrapper' before mounting on a handle of hazel wood.

Country Furniture Maker

Wilf Hutchinson, furniture maker, of Husthwaite, near Coxwold in North Yorkshire, undertaking detailed chisel work on a oak sideboard.

There is something immensely reassuring about the simple style and honest practicality of much of the furniture made over the years by country craftsmen. The use of locally-grown materials, usually oak or ash or walnut, has given a natural appearance to their work which was a result of sympathy with the wood itself as well as an understanding of the needs of the user. The local furniture maker would also be called upon to make all manner of things from farm implements to coffins. But if left to his own devices rather than distracted by fashion or fancy from London or the Continent, he would continue to make items of furniture which were simple and satisfying. The bedrock of the country furniture maker remained relatively undisturbed. Indeed in the remoter parts of the British Isles, certainly in Wales and much of Yorkshire, he retained his complete independence. The majority of his customers would have continued to call on his skills for simple, serviceable furniture, mainly in oak, no matter what their wealthier neighbours might commission from eminent architects and fashionable cabinet makers.

Yorkshire's own most famous master-craftsman in wood in recent years who stands squarely in the long line of the tradition of rural furniture making and wood-carving had the simplest of backgrounds. Robert Thompson, the 'Mouse Man' of Kilburn, was born in 1876 the son of the village joiner and wheelwright. Today his work can be seen in 700 churches throughout Britain and in homes not only in this country but overseas.

Using an adaze to fashion the surface of a piece of oak.

Robert Thompson's trade mark is a mouse. Wilf Hutchinson, one of his apprentices, chose the squirrel as his.

Walking Sticks and Shepherd's Crooks

In the old days it was the custom for farmers' sons to go into the woods on Good Friday to cut hazel for besom handles. In the late autumn or early

Fred Bentley of Rudland Farm, near Gillamoor, North Yorkshire, with a root of hazel (right) as raw material for making into a shepherd's crook.

winter they would also search the hedgerows for suitable material for making walking-sticks, thumb-sticks and shepherds' crooks. Most country folk have developed this side-line into a profitable hobby by taking it to a fine craft.

These walking sticks are usually made of hazel, which is ideal for its toughness; a few are made from holly and ash, while special sticks are made from black thorn which are rarities because the perfect piece of wood takes a lot of finding.

Fred Bentley with a variety of shepherd's crooks, walking sticks and thumb sticks which have been exhibited and sold at agricultural shows in the area.

The Cooper

The cooper is one of the most highly skilled craftsmen in wood. While cabinet-makers and joiners work precisely to written measurements and drawings, the cooper by his skill, his sense of shape and form, will produce an article which is perfectly fitted for the job it has to do. His instinct and eye alone guide the dimensions and the working angles of the constituent parts. It is an example of how the craftsman's traditional methods and materials produce a functional design which has altered little over the centuries.

In outline the making of a cask seems simple, but the skill and interest lies in the detailed workmanship and the tools which are used. A cask is made up from a number of staves or sections of wood, enclosing a circular head at either end, and bound together with steel hoops. The skill of the cooper lies chiefly in the making of the staves. Each has to be carefully shaped and bevelled with edges that are cut with the exact angle to form the tight-fitting circle of the belly of the cask. In 'trussing-up', which is another peak of his skill, the cooper will either steam the staves or heat them over a cresset or casket of fire so that they can be forced into the required shape when the hoops are put on.

A collection of tools in the cooper's shop at Masham.

Like the village smithy, the cooper's shop in a brewery is a natural focal point. People drop in to chat, to watch the cooper at work. They respect his skill. In the winter the stove, with its sweet-smelling scent of oak smoke, is a welcome comfort. His initials appearing on all the casks that pass through his hands are part of the traditional 'language' of coopers. They form a small and dwindling body of men to day. A cooper has only to see a set of initials on a cask and knows the man behind them instantly, what has happened to him, whether he is still working or has retired, or, most appropriately, is keeping a pub.

Clive Hollis, cooper at Theakston's Brewery, Masham, astride an old long jointer plane once used to shape the staves or sections of a wooden barrel before the introduction of powered machinery.

The 'inside shave' is used to obtain the correct hollowing or bow of a stave now made from Polish oak.

Fitting the final stave.

Clive Hollis hammers a rivet into a hoop on the 'bick iron'.

The 'chimb' or cap hoop is positioned with a 'driver', a flat steel wedge.

Clive Hollis makes the bung hole in the barrel with a drill and then, as seen here, a conical 'auger'.

Clogging

Older generations in Yorkshire, in mill towns and mining villages alike, will remember the distinctive sounds, particularly on early frosty mornings, of clogs on cobbles as men and women went to work. They were and still are a characteristically Northern form of footwear, probably first worn in industry by the cotton mill-workers in Lancashire although they had long been worn by farm workers. Although they later came to be regarded as a sign of poverty, with school children actively being discouraged by their teachers from wearing them, they are eminently practical and hard wearing.

Harry Greenwood, clog maker of Haworth and a familiar figure in the locality since 1925, outside his shop.

Harry Greenwood at work in his shop.

Today, clog-making gives no sign of being a dying trade in the north. Indeed, while not reaching the peaks of output during the '14-18 and '39-45 Wars when they were a vital substitute for boots and shoes, clogs play an essential role in steel-making today and in a number of other industries. Suitably fitted with 'clog irons' or special rubber layers on the sole, with toe-caps and other protective features, they are excellent for working with hot metal, damp conditions or a variety of chemicals. To the uninitiated they seem clumsy but in fact they are comfortable to wear and can be made to be absolutely water-proof. In the old days some faithful wearers even maintained that clogs possessed unique healing properties for foot ailments.

Possibly clogs were introduced into this country from the Low Countries via the Fens. By the thirteenth or fourteenth century they were worn by rich and poor alike in country districts and clog making would have been a wide-spread craft. Later the richer classes turned to more elaborate footwear. In the past, though not as numerous as cobblers, clog-makers could be found in many villages in Yorkshire.

'Butts' or 'billets' of beechwood for clog soles at F Walkley (Clogs) Limited of Hebden Bridge.

Using the traditional stock knife to fashion the clog sole from the 'butt' or 'billet' of beechwood.

The leather uppers are nailed to the clog sole before steel clog irons are fixed.

Coble Builder

Though used also by some Northumbrian fishermen, the coble is still the mainstay of the inshore fishing industry off Yorkshire's north-east coast. There are dozens of vessels owned and operated by individual fishermen which sail out of the smaller fishing ports like Staithes and Robin Hood's Bay, as well as Whitby. Building a coble seems to the uninitiated a curiously intuitive craft rather than a highly detailed technical skill. This is exactly the case. There is no

Billy Clarkson of Whitby looking at the shape and form of a coble during construction, the design of which makes for maximum seaworthiness.

such thing as a set of plans. A coble is built from experience, from knowing exactly what the fisherman wants. No doubt it comes also from the builder having observed the shape and line of the coble as a child before he starts work. Like so many other crafts, coble building has a natural law of detail and line dictated by tradition which the craftsman absorbs subconsciously, as well as by the materials used and the experience of their performance in the neighbouring fishing grounds.

A coble is clinker-built, but has no keel and its shape is all-important. Basically, it is a very good sea boat, designed with a natural logic for this particular part of the coast. No other boat in the world could withstand the weather experienced by the fishermen in the area. The coble's seaworthiness influenced Thornycroft's when they designed and built the motor torpedo boats for the last war.

Close-up of the coble's clinker-built hull showing the oak frames and the larch planking.

Although the basic shape of cobles has altered little, they have got bigger and are built with heavier timber to match the increased horse-power which owners are investing in today. This can go from 25hp up to 80hp, but always with a single screw. Today the coble is usually worked by two men, though they will sometimes take a boy along with them.

The steep rake of the coble's stern allows it to be launched stern-first into a rough sea.

39

Wool

Handloom Weavers

Handloom weaving as an integral part of the Yorkshire woollen industry is a rare phenomenon today. Usually it is an activity which is pursued by dedicated amateurs as a pastime or by creative individualists who have chosen to take up weaving as a form of therapy or escape from more mundane or demanding urban occupations. But it is ironical that the increasing rationalisation of Yorkshire's wool textile industry, brought about by modernisation and world-wide competition, should have provided an opportunity for a husband and wife team to pursue the craft of handloom weaving in a way which has a strong and continuous link with the past. They provided a service which was needed at the top end of the market in wool textiles and at the same time satisfying their own design and weaving skills.

Typical old weavers' cottages at Golcar where the upper storeys were built with a gallery of windows to give maximum light.

Keith and Margaret Brier, in a sense, are 'survivors' of the earlier domestic way of working. They worked from their home at Upperthong, above Holmfirth, in a village which was a typical setting for the cottage industry of the seventeenth and eighteenth centuries when whole families spun, wove and still farmed. Virtually every house in the village had some connection with weaving.

The Briers have designed and hand-wove short sample lengths of exclusive woollen cloths. They won orders for these designs from prestigious clothiers and stores in London and abroad which they then wove for them to the required breadth and length in their own small 'commission' mill.

Margaret Brier of Upper Thong, near Holmfirth, at work on a tappit hand loom weaving a sample length of woollen cloth.

Keith Brier preparing the warp on a warping frame for his hand loom.

Another view of Margaret Brier's tappit loom with the shuttle about to be 'thrown'

Teazling

Today Yorkshire has only one firm of teazle merchants left. Edmund Taylor (Teazles) Limited of Huddersfield are the specialist suppliers of teazle heads which are used chiefly in the West Riding woollen textile industry to raise the pile on certain kinds of cloth. The firm was established in 1849 to process and supply the curiously barbed dry seed husk of this plant which until comparatively recently was grown in Somerset and, in earlier years, in the area around Sherburn-in-Elmet in Yorkshire. Now the bulk of the teazles which are imported from Spain are sorted, prepared and supplied by Taylors direct to the woollen mills where a small number of craftsmen linger on, the teazle setters who still set them by hand into the metal frames of the traditional teazle raising machines, called 'gigs'. Taylors also cut, grade and centre drill the larger teazle heads which are used on spindle machines to raise blankets and industrial felt or impart that delicate hairy finish to cashmere or mohair knitwear.

Teazles being set by John Dodd in two rows into a 'rod' or frame at Edmund Taylor (Teazles) Limited, Green, Huddersfield. The rods are then set into a 'gig' or revolving drum at the mill across which the cloth is drawn to the 'raised' with its correct finish.

Shuttle Making

The premises of John E Fearnside at Oakworth, near Keighley, established as a shuttlemaker in 1918 in one of the wool combing centres of the worsted industry.

The traditional centres of Yorkshire's textile industry show enough ghostly hulks of former mills, which once resounded to the whirr, thump and clack of spinning frames and looms, to prove the devastating effect of world changes in textile markets. And yet the humble shuttle seems to have triumphed above all this depression, contraction as well as technological innovation. It still proves the most satisfactory method of handling yarn in a loom whether for heavy textile items like carpets or industrial belting or for certain types of fine quality woollen cloth. The wide-spread interest in hand-loom weaving has also assured the continuing life of the traditional type of shuttle in looms which are still built much according to patterns of those once used by individual workers in the weavers' cottages perched amongst the Pennines.

There is considerable skill in producing this apparently simple item which is required to travel considerable distances in a day's work to and fro across a loom. But there are few people left who know or care how to make them even though a demand still exists in this country. And old and battered shuttles, sold as 'antiques' from Yorkshire's woollen mills, find ready buyers in tourist centres like York.

Cecil Fearnside, son of the founder, planing a wooden shuttle.

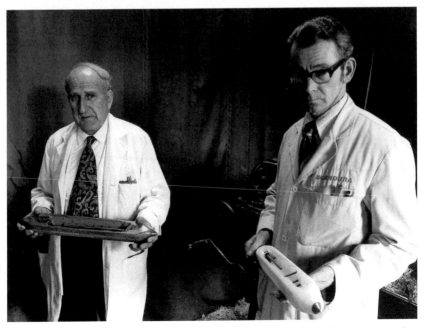

Cecil Fearnside, left, with the traditional wooden shuttle and Eric Clayton with a new type of shuttle made from polyethylene when the company joined the Scandura Group of

Tailor

Amongst the different crafts carried out in the town it is important not to forget the old-style bespoke tailor. He is the man who, by carefully, even jealously guarding his skills and carrying out the various stages in building a suit himself on his own premises, from cutting the cloth through to the final fitting, is creating something which has just as much significance and worth in terms of craftsmanship as any other hand-made item. Sadly his days as a separate, independent spirit in the provinces are numbered.

In London the famous Savile Row establishments manage to preserve their standards and talents at a price that now can only be afforded by the super-affluent. But the onslaught of the mass production 'engineering' of men's suits and also the trend towards casual leisure styles of clothing, amongst even the older generation, has put many a well-known bespoke tailor in the provinces out of business.

David Zimmerman, tailor of Stainbeck Corner, Leeds, marks with chalk a length of cloth, the first stage in making a hand tailored suit after measuring the customer.

Leeds used to be one of the most important centres for bespoke tailoring in the provinces. Like Manchester, emigré craftsmen from the Continent had brought with them to Leeds skills and experience towards the end of the nineteenth century which quickly found a growing market amongst the middle class who had grown rich by the success of the textile and engineering industries when the world was Britain's oyster. Even in the mid-thirties there were about one hundred high class bespoke tailors in Leeds. Ironically it was another 'incomer' to Leeds, Montague Burton, who helped to write their final chapter by establishing his fifty Shilling Tailors Empire.

The tailor sits on his 'board' to sew the garment.

Clay

The Potter

In the pleasantly rolling countryside around Ripon most of the villages and many of the large houses are built from a rough-textured brick that has weathered into a particularly mellow tint of reddish-brown. Many of the buildings in Ripon itself, in the shadow of the great cathedral, have been built from the same brick that once was the product of a thriving industry in the district. In its hey-day at the turn of the century a series of small brickworks, producing hand-made bricks from the excellent local clay, provided work for a hundred men or more. They were employed in brickworks at Roecliffe, Littlethorpe, and on the Newby Estate itself. These small brickworks, which also produced tiles and a range of heavy domestic and horticultural pottery, were part of a tradition of craftsmanship which stretched back over 200 years.

Roly Curtis, of Littlethorpe Potteries near Ripon, North Yorkshire, puts pots to dry 'white' on a heated bench before firing in the kiln – a process which can take up to a week.

Making a panchion on the wheel from clay dug from a nearby site.

Roly Curtis places pots of various types into an electric kiln which takes 24 hours to fire and 48 hours to cool down.

Straw, Willow and Fibre

Crab Pots

It is not really surprising that something as traditional and old as fishing should have such items which depend on individual skill and reliability in their creation. Just as most of the inshore fishermen working off Yorkshire's north-east coast are their own masters, owning their own boats, beholden to no-one else in anonymous authority, so the people who supply them with many of their needs tend to be in a similarly independent position. Deep sea and middle water fishing today demands the investment of the large fishing companies who may in turn be linked to larger, more distant corporations, with the back-up of the latest and most sophisticated navigational and fish detection aids. But the inshore fisherman working out of Staithes or Whitby or Scarborough is thoroughly independent, with only the elements and the sea itself to contend with. It is noticeable that they are more resourceful than their deep sea brothers. They have to be for financial reasons and because they prefer to trust things that they have either made themselves or which have been made for them by trusted craftsmen.

The crab and lobster pots they use are typical examples of this traditional approach towards their fishing gear. The design and methods of making have altered little over the years. In some areas a basket-work, bell-like pot trap is used, usually in the West Country. But in Yorkshire the traps are essentially simple half circle tunnels of wood and netting fixed to a wooden base which lie upon the bed of the sea in the fisherman's favourite places just off the coast.

Willie Wright, a fisherman at Staithes, with one of the crab pots made to use in inshore waters.

Thatcher

Thatch in Yorkshire is something of a curiosity amongst the stone or red-tiled roofs. So one might be forgiven for not regarding thatching as a traditional craft in this part of England, unlike the Midlands or the West Country where so many villages seem to burgeon with thatched roofs. But before stone or slate or tile, thatch was the universal roof covering throughout Yorkshire. Sometimes on an old cottage you may see the ghostly traces of the former type of roof. The pitch of a thatched roof has to be much steeper to allow the rain to flow off quickly whereas a stone or tiled roof is more shallow. So you will see where new stone or brick has been added at a later date at the gable end to accommodate the new type of roof. The steeper pitch still may remain as a shadowy profile

Seth Eccles of Helmsley thatching a cruck-house at the Ryedale Folk Museum, Hutton-le-Hole, using the long straw method.

A 'spit' of hazel secures the 'yealmes' of straw and iron bodkins stitch the straw to the frame of the roof with twine.

Basket Maker

The actual method of making a basket is in essence very simple. But the interest lies in the fact that basket making is one of the oldest crafts in existence and that there is a direct continuity stretching back over the centuries to earlier primitive communities where baskets were an essential element in existence. Even in Roman times, British made baskets were well known for their strength, shape and durability.

Willow rods are used, whether for baskets, furniture or fencing, in their brown or original state, that is with the skin or bark still intact or stripped 'white' or 'buff'. In the latter case the rods are first boiled in a tank and then stripped. The dye out of the skin turns the rod a pleasant, mellow buff colour. If you require rods to be used 'white' these have to be peeled while they are still wet with sap from cutting. The bulk of the willow used is left 'brown' and after cutting care is taken to see that the rods are left to dry out thoroughly before they are stacked under cover.

In the past, basket-making became an industry. Standard items were made in hundreds. There was a large basket-making industry in Leeds making nothing else but mill skeps for the textile industry. That has all gone now. Today

The tools used in basket making, included bodkin, flat hammer, picking knife, curved knife, shears and the 'plank' on which the basket is worked.

basket-making has returned to a craft activity with individuals doing it or small groups who tend to make more individual items.

John Taylor, of Ulleskelf near Selby, North Yorkshire, makes a basket from willow grown on the family's land nearby.

Ropes and Nets

S mall or single-man fibre rope-making businesses were as closely in touch with the needs of farmers as ropemakers in ports were with those of a shipping or fishing industry still largely powered by sail. You have only to notice the number of streets or lanes in towns and villages with names like The Ropewalk, Rope Street or Ropemaker Street to realise the former extent of this traditional craft industry.

Spinning up the three strands to make the completed rope using the wooden 'top', in the foreground.

Fibre rope and twine are still used extensively on the land. Whereas in the past rope was mainly used for lines for working with plough horses or for tying down wagon-loads of hay, its use today is perhaps more specialised, for example as cow bands used in modern milking parlours. Changing patterns of demand, as well as the growth of larger rope-making companies and the introduction of new, man-made materials into the industry in place of traditional, natural fibres hastened the disappearance of the small country ropemaker. Fortunately, the few who remain are surprisingly vigorous because of a recent revival of interest in the activity and its products by the general public.

Peter Annison, once a Polytechnic lecturer in textiles who took over the old-established business of W R Outhwaite & Son, of Hawes in Wensleydale, 'warps up' with cotton yarn to make the strand as the first stage in rope making.

Changes have also affected the country netmaker but the situation is not so healthy here. Netting is either made in distant factories or imported. The needs of the majority of farmers have changed too. Hay or straw is usually stored in the new, gaunt concrete barns and wire netting has tended to supersede fibre materials for the control of live-stock.

So the country netmaker today is a rare figure indeed. But old ways persist in remote country districts of Yorkshire. There is still a demand amongst some farmers for net and netting made in the old way. There is enough work to keep one man busy, maybe. As a traditional rural craft it is still alive, but only just.

Allan Addy of Westgate, Driffield, filling a netting needle with coir yarn.

Making a diamond mesh stack net using the needle and mesh or 'mash' board, in Allan Addy's right hand.

55

Corn Dollies

The corn dolly is known variously in different parts of the country as corn mother, mell baby, corn baby, kirn child, kirn doll and mell mother. But the corn dolly must not be confused with the ornaments which used to be placed on the thatching of hay and straw ricks. These are merely bound into crude shapes and not plaited like the corn dolly.

Sidney Beeforth of Westerdale, in the North York Moors, makes a corn dolly from hollow-stemmed straw grown specially for his craft.

What is perhaps confusing is the word 'dolly'. Most probably it derives from idol rather than a child's doll though it is from the distant myths and legends that the custom sprang most generally of fashioning the carefully preserved last stalks of corn form the field into the shape of a woman - an idol to Ceres? - the corn dolly which was then carried to the farmhouse and displayed on the wall during the festivities at the end of the harvest. She was kept until the sowing of next year's seed corn and again offering thanks when all the harvest was safely gathered in. Today it is merely left for us to appreciate the simple designs which have been created out of a natural material that has come from the land. The corn dolly bought during a country holiday and then hung up at home seems to retain something of the quintessence of the harvest cycle in a way which is sympathetic and comfortingly genuine.

Mr and Mrs Beeforth with their handiwork used for talks and demonstrations in the area.

Metal

Blacksmith and Farrier

There is a blacksmith and there is a farrier or shoeing-smith; the two craftsmen should not be confused. The blacksmith has always regarded his craft as being one of the oldest. The discovery of the art of metal working was one of man's most important. Used for ornaments at first, once its smelting was fully understood, iron quickly took over from bronze and became the preferred metal for weapons and tools. Because he made almost everything needed for the community for use in the home, on the land or to wage war, the blacksmith was regarded as the king among craftsmen, in rural communities which were formerly self-sufficient.

George Twiddle, a traditional country blacksmith, at Brigham near Driffield, outside his smithy, reputed to be well over 250 years old, with one of his farrows.

The shoeing-smith appeared on the scene later. Before the days of made-up roads it was not essential to shoe horses. Later the need developed and the men who specialised in this work were called farriers, derived from the Latin *'faber farrarius'* (or 'one skilful in iron work'). The blacksmith was the worker in iron, smithing or 'smiting' implements and iron-work generally. The farrier made the shoes and shod the horses, whether for working on the land or for riding and hunting, and as the horse population grew he became too busy to do anything else except act as a horse doctor until the veterinary surgeon appeared.

However, there has always been much overlapping of work, particularly in the country where the craftsman has always had to be versatile, ready to mend a broken plough one day and shoe a horse or pony the next. When the use of horses on the land declined after the last war many a farrier, to make a living, became a general smith and agricultural engineer. But as the interest in riding horses has revived so once again he has become the specialist with modern, portable equipment, going out to work at stables rather than having his customers come to the forge.

Today, with the sweeping mechanisation of the land, inevitably the traditional type of country blacksmith, too, has had to adapt, to develop into an agricultural engineer as familiar with the latest refinements of gas or electrical welding as he has been with the mastery of the hearth.

Heating up the iron in the hearth, with the degree of heat being judged by the blacksmith's eye alone.

George Twiddle at work on his single-ended anvil in his small, crowded smithy.

Robert Leete, a young blacksmith at Helmsley Forge, has created much fine wrought ironwork.

Robert Leete making a wrought-iron scroll.

Phil Dowson, the fourth generation of a Kirkbymoorside family as a farrier to run the Ryedale Forge, with a background of sets of old shoes used as patterns for each horse shod.

Nailing a hind shoe.

61

Dales Tinsmith

The tinsmith was an essential craftsman in any country area simply because of the wide variety of cans and vessels which were needed for daily use on a farm. In some places this would be carried out by a travelling tinker who would carry his tools on his back and set up his workshop at the corner of a farmyard or on the road-side, using a peat fire to provide the necessary heat to work with.

Though the principle of tinning wrought iron sheets was well known before, it was not until the eighteenth century that new methods were introduced to improve the iron, the rolling and the tinning. The nineteenth century was the great period of technical development of the industry. At its beginning, relatively heavy gauge and small-sized wrought iron sheets were being tinned by hand dipping. At its end, light-gauge open-hearth steel sheets were being tinned in mechanical units at speeds of over one hundred inches per minute.

The wider availability of cheaper material was a boon to tinsmiths and their wares found wider and wider custom. It proved to be a reliable and versatile material where its anti-corrosive properties were necessary. In particular it satisfied the needs of Dales farmers with their herds of cows grazing in the summer in upper pastures on the fell sides. Indeed the variety of vessels

Cuthbert Croft, who formerly ran a family tinsmith's business in Reeth in Swaledale which was established in the 18th century, at work on the 'stake' or tinsmith's anvil.

used in the sequence of collecting and distributing milk, right through from the milking of the cow to delivery it to the housewife in the village, is a useful description of the range of the tinsmith's work.

A collection of tinsmith's tools owned by Cuthbert Croft now displayed in the Swaledale Folk Museum at Reeth.

Making a seam for a tin vessel.

Leather

Saddlers

Tom Thacker, a general saddler in the market town of Bedale, measures a leather horse collar.

The work now done on saddlery for working horses on the land is a rare occurrence for a craftsman.

In the past there was a distinct pattern to the year for a saddler or harness-maker. January and February were the quietest months of the year when horse collars were made for stock. From March to May a lot of 'gear' was supplied to farmers for the busy seed-sowing period, after ploughing and harrowing. Then June and July were a little quieter for sales of 'gear', but there was in its place a lot of work repairing old canvasses or fitting new ones for the binding machines for harvest time. At harvest time in August or September the work on these rose to a crescendo; they shrank if the weather was wet and then the farmers needed urgent help with the repair in mid-field. In September and October the emphasis turned more on getting 'tack' ready for the hunting season.

Sadly today a saddlery is mainly concerned with repairs and miscellaneous leather work rather than with new work. But considering the number of different jobs a typical saddlery is still called upon to do, the range of tools is surprisingly small. Probably the bare minimum could be listed as the needle, the hand knife and the round knife but you would see many more in the average saddlers: a whole range of awls and needles, the prick irons, the palm or hand iron which pushes or pulls the needle through the leather and the plough

Malcolm , a self-taught saddler near Malton, has successfully developed his business by offering his skills to racing stables in North Yorkshire. Here he is making the saddle-tree which is the frame on which the light-weight racing saddle is later built.

gauge which is used to cut out long lengths of leather in strips of predetermined width for making up bridles, reins, girth straps and traces.

Just as the wagoner and the ploughman in the past depended on the harness-maker's skill, so the rider today whether hacking or hunting still depends on the saddler's craftsmanship. But no rider is more dependent than the racing jockey. The racing saddler provides a standard of workmanship which must match the thoroughbred qualities of the animals wearing the gear he makes.

As well as being the sport of kings, horse racing is meat and drink to many a Yorkshireman. The country abounds with race courses from the small and cosy like Thirsk to the large and hectic like York or Doncaster, home of the Leger. Behind this sport exists an industry well equipped to service its every need. In North Yorkshire in particular there are stud farms and trainers each with distinctive reputations and skills for breeding and raising horses which provide profit and thrills at many race meetings in and beyond Yorkshire.

The component parts of a racing saddle.

Village Bootmaker

In the past most sizeable Yorkshire villages, with 300 inhabitants or more, would have been able to support a cobbler or bootmaker. Rough stone roads and the daily wear and tear of working on the land in all weathers would have provided ample work for a man who could make new boots and repair the old. To the average farmer a stout pair of boots would have been as important as the way his horses were shod. The village bootmaker would have occupied as prominent and necessary a position in the local community as the blacksmith.

Frank Ward, who described himself as a 'practical bootmaker', in his workroom behind his shop in Leyburn, stitching the sole of an upper, using in his right hand a curved awl.

But today the few bootmakers who still exist in Yorkshire no longer can afford the time to make new boots or shoes even if people were prepared to pay their prices for the genuine, hand-made article. Most of these craftsmen are now in the towns and even they are only concerned with repair work. Genuine hand-made footwear is a rarity indeed. Even the majority of so-called hand-made shoes sold in London by established names in the industry, though made to an individual last or pattern for the owner, are machine-sewn rather than hand-sewn. In any case the concept of a pair of shoes or a pair of boots being bought and made to last, treated with respect and care, and repaired time and time again, has become a quaint anachronism in the face of the modern shoe industry's high-pressure marketing techniques, the continual and often fey changes of fashion enflamed by advertising. Maybe soon shoes will become disposables, not even worth the price of repairing - and many a surviving craftsman will not have even that work to keep him going.

Some of the tools of the bootmaker's craft - hack-knife, gripper, pliers, fudge-wheel for finishing the welt, file and curved awl.

Frank Ward burnishes a sole.

The 'Little Mesters' of Sheffield

The 'little mesters' who still exist in Sheffield with surprising resilience, despite the formidable difficulties facing the cutlery trade because of fierce foreign competition, are the successors of workers in those nineteenth century interdependent cottage industries, based on the traditional system of outwork known in the town as 'liver and draw' - hand in the goods and get the cash. No matter what specialised need arises there seems to be a one or two man business to supply this - to a very high standard of skill and quality. All over Sheffield there are men whose talents are seldom recorded, working with antiquated equipment or machinery of the simplest kind adapted for its particular purpose with great ingenuity, in premises which must cause disquiet to many a factory inspector. Yet such is the skill and enterprise of these craftsmen that their safety records today are high and the job satisfaction even higher.

Sheffield's continuing variety of skills in the cutlery trade are too numerous to be adequately described here. But there are several main areas which best illustrate the fine traditions - for example, the hand forging of knife blades, blade grinding and the work of the cutler. Fortunately there are still a few 'little mesters' left who can illustrate these skills but when this generation retires who will follow them? At last it appears that a continuity stretching from the fourteenth century in Hallamshire may finally end.

George Watt's forging shop, hidden away in a small courtyard off Broomspring Lane, Sheffield, was probably the city's last knife-blade forger.

Knife Blade Forger

Now that the vast proportion of knives and other tools with cutting edges are machine stamped in what remains of the Sheffield Cutlery trade today the hand forging of blades is a rare craft indeed.

Those who value a knife as a reliable cutting tool will affirm that the hand-forged blade has a far superior and longer-lasting edge than drop-stamped or mass-produced blades. Hand-forging ensures that the granular structure of the steel is very compact so when the blade is hardened a superior quality is given to it.

According to Abel Bywater's 'Sheffield Dialect' published in 1839 the blade forger has four steps or stages in his work which are the same today as when described: '1st he moodst blades', Bywater says, '2nd he tangs it, 3rd he smithies it and 4th he hardens an' tempers it and then he's done w't.'

The knife forger's coke-fired hearth, smaller than a blacksmith's, is fronted by a thick steel plate on which the blades are tapped when taken from the fire to dislodge coke and scale.

George Watts' 'stiddy' or anvil for the 'hitting' of blades lying immediately under a south-facing window.

Grinder

The grinders in the Sheffield cutlery trade form an important bridge between the hand blade forgers and the cutlers who fit the knives together. They are the men who produce the cutting edge. Most of the grinding is done today by the big cutlery manufacturers on a factory basis but as with so much that is made in the trade in Sheffield there is still a constant demand for the specialised item, for that extra quality of craftsmanship which can only be produced by the 'little mesters', the independent man working for himself who can tackle the widely different mix of products which would confound any factory production manager with cost accountants breathing down his neck.

A handful of finished ground knife-blades.

Rowland Swindon rented a small part of Granville Works in Arundel Street, in Sheffield's former cutlery district, where other craftsmen worked, for grinding knife-blades on a water-cooled composite grindstone.

Penknife Cutler

The term 'cutler' is often wrongly used to describe collectively the craftsmen who make the various items in Sheffield's cutlery trade. It actually refers very specifically to those who do the work of building up and putting handles to knife blades. The cutler completes the construction of the finished article, such as a pen or pocket knife. In his hands the skill of the blade forger and the grinder achieves full expression. Cutlers in fact tend to divide themselves into sub-groups such as 'pocket knife cutler'. Cutler can also describe the work of the table knife 'hafter', the scissors 'work-board hand' and, until recently, the razor 'haftor'.

'Penknife' describes a whole range of small knives with spring-folding blades today which are still closely associated with Sheffield. Originally it was used specifically to describe a knife with a slender and very delicate blade designed for cutting and shaping a quill to form a pen. The wing feathers of geese usually provided the quills. Although they were sold in large quantities ready cut for the writer, many people preferred to make and renew their own pens, which explained the enormous demand for these knives from the early eighteenth century to about 1900. The quill was superseded by the steel nib and the fountain pen.

Eric Wragg worked in a small workshop high above West Street in Sheffield as a cutler specialising in making penknives.

Close-up of a fully equipped penknife with each of the tools being hand-made by Eric Wragg before assembly.

Silversmith

While London silversmiths chose to continue a tradition of handworking in silver, which had begun centuries before Sheffield's entry into the craft, silverware producers in Sheffield turned out pieces in quantity which had a considerable uniformity in appearance.

Not surprisingly, this mass production approach brought considerable prosperity to the firms which grew on the success of the sales of their silverware to the growing middle classes, conscious of their new status in Victorian England. But real inspiration and craftsmanship were lacking. By the end of the 19th century the large quantity of poorly-designed, mass-produced silverware stimulated a healthy reaction amongst a small group of silversmiths in Sheffield. Under the influence of a number of silversmiths who have trained at the Sheffield School of Art a new and higher standard of work has developed today. Such work is becoming more and more widely known and Sheffield, which formerly chose to adopt mass-production techniques for silversmithing, is gaining a new reputation for fine hand-made silverware ranging from flatware to jewellery.

Jack Spencer, a designer-silversmith of Ecclesall Road, Sheffield, uses a double-ended hammer to 'block out' a disc of sterling silver on a silversmith's leather-covered sandbag as the first stage in hand raising a silver goblet.

Subsequent 'courses' or stages in the making of a goblet are 'raised' or worked on the silversmith's anvil, with annealing taking place between 'courses' to prevent the silver hardening and cracking.

Horn Cutters

Side by side with Sheffield's cutlery trade are a number of other related crafts which have played a part in the total picture of the diversity and interdependence of the traditional industries in the city. The horn trade is typical. It grew alongside the cutlery trade in supplying it with material for knife handles and 'scales' or coverings for pen and pocket-knives. But at the same time the horn cutters could do considerable additional business in making handles for riding crops and whips, handles for drinking tankards and sections for fancy billiard cues.

Bernard Whiting and Harry Scarlett, formerly of Rocking Street, Sheffield were the last of the industry's horn cutters in the city. Their raw materials would include two types of buffalo horn.

English oxen and cattle would have provided Sheffield craftsmen with horn even in Chaucer's day. It is likely that the famous 'Sheffield thwitel' or meat knife carried by his Miller of Trumpington and now almost a symbol of the cutlery trade would have had a haft or handle of horn. Even then horn-cutters would have had extra business by making lanthorns. They would split ox-horn into fine layers which being firm as well as transparent for a candle's flame would light many on their way. Sadly, plastics have made massive inroads into the requirements of Sheffield cutlers for cut horn for handles and scales.

Bernard Whiting at his cutting wheel.

Harry Scarlett holds a knife fitted with a deer horn handle.

Mother-of-Pearl

Mother-of-Pearl has long been a material associated with Sheffield's craftsmen. It is another example of an item, specialised and distinctive enough still to be in demand, which is supplied to the cutlery industry for handles for knives and forks. But the pearl shell, with skilled cutting and handling, is capable of being used for a host of other purposes: for spoons, buttons and beads. Furthermore the material is handled with such skill that very little of it is wasted.

H A Gillott, a member of the family firm of W Gillott and Son, The Pearl Works in Eyre Lane, Sheffield, making the first cut in a shell using a water-cooled circular diamond edge cutting wheel.

The use of shell for handles by the cutlery trade as it developed in Sheffield during the eighteenth century was a predictable enough development as more elegant knives and forks were used by the gentry and the aspiring middle classes. Today, for cutlery handles of quality and elegance, it is still used despite the encroachment of all manner of plastic materials. The mother-of-pearl trade still manages to exist, although, with the escalating cost and the difficulties of finding suitable shell, the problems are considerable.

The pearl cutter sitting at his bench in front of a window, with the help of a bright light, depends on finger skill to aid his judgement in assessing the thickness of the shell to produce the required 'slabs' or blanks for knife handles.

John Gillott grinding 'slabs' of Mother-of-pearl on a carborundum wheel.

Ecclesiastical Crafts

Master Mason

Usually in the shadow of a great cathedral, within easy distance of its stonework, you will find the mason's workshop. There you will see stone in various stages of working, great blocks of limestone waiting the attention of the sawyer, a piece of half-completed tracery for a window, or a grinning gargoyle with one wing carved and the other waiting the detail of fine chisel work. From these workshops comes the love of working in stone to protect and refurbish the craftsmanship of previous generations of stone masons who have built a wonderful fabric to the greater glory of God. But today the skill goes into preservation rather than creation though who can deny the skill and dedication of the men who work to guard and repair original and priceless workmanship, often on slender and increasingly precarious budgets, which more and more is endangered by vibration and pollution generated by twentieth century affluence?

It is no slur on the ability or position of the master mason today to say that he is no longer the man he was when cathedrals like York or Beverley or Ripon were built. It is merely that he has a different responsibility. In the great days of cathedral creation the master mason was they key figure. He was the architect upon whose shoulders rested the responsibility for not only the great vision of the building but also its substance. He translated ideas and plans into stone, wood and stained glass. He headed a great team of dedicated craftsmen: the stone masons, the wood carvers, the glaziers. He was the unifying factor and it is ironic that these supremely gifted men of imagination and management skill usually have passed unknown by name into history. But who need worry about his name being remembered when he has a whole cathedral as his signature?

Jack Yarker, a former master mason in charge of the stone fabric of Ripon Minster, at work on a gargoyle to replace one of the originals.

78

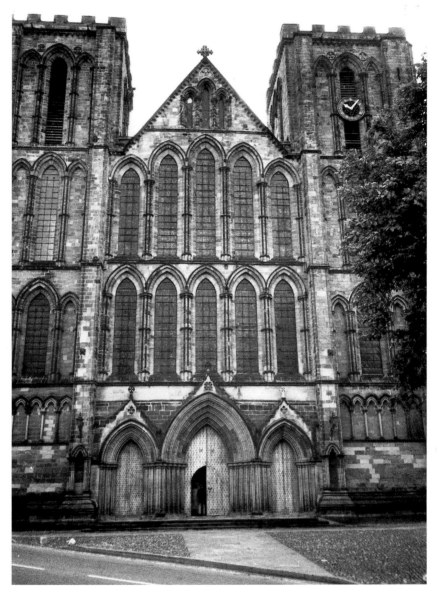

The west face of Ripon Minster, showing the intricacy and expanse of stone-work to be inspected and maintained by the master mason.

Glazier

Of all the crafts that have existed since medieval times none can be as brilliant and unique as the work carried out by medieval glass painters in stained glass. As a result of their genius and hard work, York today has the largest accumulated collection of ancient stained and painted glass in England, not only visible in the surviving handful of York's forty-one medieval parish churches but in the glory of York Minster, Britain's largest cathedral and the

Peter Gibson, former company secretary and superintendent of the York Glaziers' Trust, which was established in 1966, has prime responsibility for preserving and restoring all the stained glass in York Minster and other Christian churches or notable buildings in this country.

North country's supreme achievement in stone, the work of two and a half centuries, from 1220 until 1472. The Minster itself is the largest single concentration of glass painting of every century form the twelfth to the twentieth. Combining brilliance of beauty with reverence and mystery, the work of scores of glazier craftsmen, most of whom are unknown, it is a complete visual commentary on glass painting over eight hundred years.

A remarkable continuum of glazing craftsmanship still persists in York today, not only in the contemporary glass painters who live and work in the city, amongst whom possibly the most distinguished is Harry Harvey, but also embodied in the existence of the York Glazier's Trust. This unique body was established in 1966 and registered as a company in 1967, its trustees being nominated by the Dean and Chapter of York and the Pilgrim Trust, serving under the chairmanship of the Dean of York.

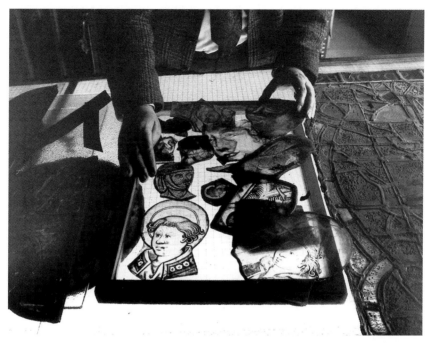

Examining over a special light table pieces of medieval glass, which are kept in the York Glaziers' Trust 'bank', carefully indexed according to age or design for use in replacing worn or broken glass in a window.

A lead 'came' of 'H' section of lead being opened out with a 'lathekin' to receive glass.

Clockmakers

Side by side with commercial prosperity came the development of local government in England. The municipalisation of the English town spread swiftly in the second half of the nineteenth century. West Riding woollen towns, the growing cities of Leeds and Sheffield, backed by the prosperity of developing manufacturing and engineering industries, embarked on creating civic buildings of great and often pompous splendour to impress both locals and visiting dignitaries. This was a busy and prosperous time not only for architects, builders and suppliers as the fabric of municipal buildings rose across the Yorkshire townscape, but also for men in many attendant crafts and skills. Masons and glaziers and joiners found new outlets as did more specialist workers, such as clockmakers. Indeed no civic building could be considered complete without its clocktower.

Two other ready outlets for public clocks were parish churches and the railways. Whenever a new parish church was commissioned it was customary for the firm of clockmakers to produce a special brochure which was used to canvass for further business. In addition to lengthy lists of all the clocks which the firm had completed throughout the whole country as well as the North (and in later years, by way of export to certain parts of the Empire), there were extracts of the reports on the new clock which appeared in the local Press.

Though clockmaking today is a far cry from the great and stately days when individual craftsmen were commissioned by individual patrons rather than municipalities, institutions and other assorted anonymous bodies to produce a clock of size and significance, there are still many elements of craftsmanship which are demanded even by newer materials. Versatility is still a necessary attribute, too.

Jim Fewster, at the works of Wm Potts and Sons in Cookridge Street, Leeds, painting in the numerals of a clock face destined for a village church or public building.

Domestic and Decorative

Knitting

The making of 'ganseys', the knitting of guernseys or jerseys, is still continued by the womenfolk in the villages along Yorkshire's north-east coast. The style and terminology associated with these knitted garments seems to have originated in the Channel Islands, where the knitting of stockings was the islands' chief export industry in the sixteenth century. The industry was so important that the islanders were evidently given special import licences to ship in wool to augment the supply of wool from local sheep. A further boost to the prosperity of the industry was given when Sir Walter Raleigh was Governor of Jersey from 1600 to 1603. He established trade between his island and Newfoundland which aided the shipbuilding industry and also, as a consequence, the demand for woollen garments by the sailors. The local inhabitants knitted with such application and industry that in 1608 a law had to be passed to forbid anyone over the age of fourteen knitting during harvest-time. Woollen garments for sailors and fishermen came to replace sealskin clothing as the seals became harder to obtain around the coasts of Britain. Wool was recognised as being a hardwearing and water-repellent material and so guernseys and jerseys also took on their own identities; 'ganseys' with their thick, heavy dark-blue wool and jerseys for their lighter, thinner yarns and wider variety of colours. The close links between Jersey and Newfoundland meant that jerseys were more popular and common than guernseys or ganseys. But ganseys came to be knitted in increasing quantities in the north of England and Scotland where their warmth and serviceability were widely appreciated amongst the fishing community.

Mrs Ethel Richardson, of Old Whitby, a fisherman's wife, using the traditional four needles to knit a 'gansey'.

Rug-prodding

Prod-rugs are a typical feature of domestic handiwork in Yorkshire. These prod-rugs, also known as 'piece', 'peg', or 'peggie' rugs, consist of mixed and colourful clips of cloth which are prodded into a piece of hessian. Warm, long-lasting and bright, they are now much sought-after, often fetching quite high prices second-hand at sales of household belongings. Perhaps a predictable by-product of the wool textile industry, originally introduced through the 'fent' sellers who sold off the cuts and left-overs from the weaving mills, they are an example of Yorkshire thrift and practical good sense. Today they make use of all manner of clippings of old clothes and other cloth remnants. They are still to be seen on floors in many Dales homes. Their deep and cushiony pile make them ideal for any stone or tile floors. Children and pets find them irresistible to lie on in front of an open fire. With a cheerful, casual, almost accidental pattern and bright colours, they provided a modest creative outlet for farmers' wives in the past, who found themselves tied to their homes during the winter in pre-television days. In the old days in the Dales a new prod-rug put down upon the floor was almost a custom after the spring clean was done.

The 'Rug-prodders of Arkengarthdale', ten ladies who have made 'prod' or 'peg' rugs of 'clips' of cloth prodded into a hessian backing over many years in aid of chapel funds in Langthwaite.

*Mrs Nellie Hird (left) known as 'the gaffer', and a former leading light of the 'rug-prodders',
who also used to cut the 'clips' of cloth, about two stone being necessary for a full-sized 'prod'
rug.*

Lace

Pillow lace-making was once known as 'bone lace' because the actual bobbins used in making it were carved or turned from bone or because the pattern was followed by means of fishbones as pins. Later this type of lace-making came to be referred to as 'bobbin lace' because of the bobbins used as compared with needle-point lace which is made upon a cloth foundation and which has never really been popular in this country. Latterly, it has been usual to refer to it as 'pillow lace' because of the various types of specially stuffed pillows which are used to support the pattern and the pins which hold the threads while the lace maker follows the pattern.

Essentially a cottage industry to provide a little extra money for families, lace-making has always been at the mercy of either fashion or competition from the Continent or from machines. References in the 17th century and 18th century to lace-making make it appear that it was taught in either workhouse or in 'lace schools', providing an intensive activity that produced very little return for those engaged in it.

Close-up of the lace pattern as it develops on the 'pillow' with the threads of linen yarn running from the bobbins to the pins holding the stitches in place, the complexity of the pattern being decided by the number of bobbins.

But as with so many other crafts in this country it was the development of lace-making by machinery during the 19th century that killed off the activity associated with small country communities, providing a thin barrier against poverty.

Mrs Florence Longman, of Wombleton near Helmsley, making a 'pillow' lace.

Quilting

Plain quilts consisting of whole cloth top and back, sandwiching an inner layer of wadding, the decoration being provided by the stitching, consisting of simple designs taken from everyday items, seem to be of fairly early origin. The patchwork type of quilting where shapes from different pieces of material are applied or stitched down upon the whole cloth top, or alternatively, stitched together to form a larger piece of textile, may well be of later origin as more fanciful designs of woven textiles became more widely available.

The influence of quilt-making in County Durham upon neighbouring Swaledale in Yorkshire was natural. Swaledale quilting has been of a fairly distinctive type, being mainly of the plain quilt type rather than patchwork. The decoration is added by means of the actual quilting patterns stitched rather than the textiles used. These are based on simple shapes: a chain border, a fern, a star with a wild dog-rose in its centre, feathers, the Prince of Wales feather, tulips in a plant pot, a fan and a diamond stitching which forms a background pattern, with a circular border pattern made with a cup.

Though Swaledale quilts are prized as part of a wedding trousseau or family heirloom they no longer seem to be made in the area. The sad decline of this decorative and useful domestic craft has been caused by the wide-spread popularity, stimulated by heavy advertising, of the duvet or Continental quilt.

Miss Annie Pickard of Kirkbymoorside with her patchwork quilt containing over three thousand hexagonal patches of different print material, made on a wooden frame in her front parlour

Part of a traditional North Country quilt, of a type made in Swaledale or County Durham, showing the hand-stitched patterning which also holds the 'wadding' between two layers of cloth.

Farmhouse Cheese

Is farmhouse cheese-making a craft or an art? Whichever way you look at it the white soft curd cheeses for which North Yorkshire is famous, particularly those made in Wensleydale, are still made today by farmers' wives with milk warm from the cow. There are not many of them but enough to keep one of the old traditional mainstays of the farmer's diet alive. However, since the war and stringent hygiene controls laid down by the Milk Marketing Board, these cheeses cannot be sold - at least on the open market though rumour has it that some of these cheeses are for sale to a few, select customers who know how to keep a secret.

Today the bulk of the famous Wensleydale cheese is made in a factory - the majority of the white in Hawes and the delectable blue, which many prefer to blue Stilton, now alas made outside Yorkshire. White and blue cannot usually be made in the same factory because otherwise the bacteria needed to create the flavoursome characteristic mould would spread to affect the white.

It is similar in appearance, though not altogether in taste, to Caerphilly cheese. Just as this came to be an essential part of the Welsh coal miner's diet, so Wensleydale cheese, as this cheese has come to be known from the whole area, (since the cheese fairs were established in Leyburn in the 1840's) is a favourite not only with South Yorkshire miners but with farm families and those who come to help them at harvest time. Then it is eaten with traditional wheat cakes.

Mrs Margery Stones, a farmer's wife in Arkengarthdale and one of the few people in the Yorkshire Dales to make cheese of the white Wensleydale type in her home for family and friends, using her old cheese-press.

The size of the finished cheese depends on how much cream there is in the milk.

Staithes Bonnets

That curiously distinctive and charmingly anachronistic style of women's headgear in North-east Yorkshire known as the Staithes Bonnet, derived from the traditional Yorkshire bonnet. It looks rather like a cross between a sou'wester and a mob cap. If you look at some of the photographs taken by Sutcliffe of Whitby at the turn of the century you will notice that most of the women are wearing them. Indeed they were worn by the womenfolk of the fishing community in particular, being developed as a kind of protective head-dress, when carrying in the dripping baskets full of the day's catch on their head or the coils of fishing lines for their menfolk who manned the famous Yorkshire coble fishing boats in all weathers. The crown of the bonnet is padded to protect the head and the long frill at the back is intended to prevent the drips of water running down the neck.

But the Staithes Bonnet has for many years been something more than a protective covering for the head. It has been a touch of ritual in Staithes itself and to a certain degree in the other fishing villages up and down the coast in the area. It used to be made and worn regularly in three colours, each with a prime

significance: black for mourning, lilac for half-mourning (after one year), print for a weekday bonnet and a plain white bonnet for Sunday best.

Today there are only a few left in Staithes who still wear the bonnet, though quite a few still know how to make them from patterns which are handed down carefully from mother to daughter or via close friends, and these are mainly elderly folk.

Miss Harriet Anderson, maker of Staithes bonnets since she was a child, had the honour of having one of hers accepted by the Queen in 1974 as a gift from the Staithes Ladies Lifeboat Guild to mark the 150th anniversary of the Royal National Lifeboat Institution.

Jet Carving

Whitby jet is one of Yorkshire's geological peculiarities and jet carving is a craft which Whitby has made all its own. Said to be the oldest industry in that part of the North York moors, jet working was active in the Bronze Age and continued through the Roman occupation into the Middle Ages.

The revival of the jet trade in modern times was the idea of a retired naval man, Captain Tremlett, who was interested in turning amber beads into a hobby. In 1800 two Whitby men, John Carter and Robert Jefferson, started making objects out of jet, including crosses and beads, for sale to visitors to the town. Soon after this other workshops opened in lanes and alleyways behind the main streets. Queen Victoria is usually given the credit for turning jet into a fashion craze after introducing it into her court, and after Prince Albert died in 1861 jet ornaments were worn as a token of the nation's mourning. Yet the showing of a number of examples of jet craftsmanship at the Great Exhibition at the Crystal palace in 1851 must certainly have given a boost to the Whitby trade.

By the end of the nineteenth century the craze had died away. Changing fashions, and the difficulty of finding enough suitable material to work with, had brought the industry almost to a finish. In the 'twenties not more than 40 men were employed and by the mid-thirties a mere half dozen were left. The long line of tradition in the craft seemed likely to break completely. No apprentices were articled to the remaining craftsmen. Yet, with the surprising capacity of crafts to show a sudden resilience when all the signs point towards extinction, there is still one apprenticed jet craftsman now at work in Whitby.

Roy Jay, a craftsman apprenticed in long tradition, carves jet jewellery in his workshop above Church Street in Old Whitby.

Sport and Leisure

Cricket Bats

In the past, Yorkshire players, professional or amateur, whether in test matches or in the multitude of inter-village leagues, could buy their cricket bats knowing that these came from craftsmen who would lovingly fashion them by hand from start to finish. These followed a tradition of bat-making dating from the late eighteenth century when a standard width of $4^3/_4$ inches was established.

Apart from a scattering of individual craftsmen in different parts of the country, today's bat is much more a factory-made, mass-produced article, possibly more in keeping with the more intensive pace of contemporary cricket. Even so, some professionals have been known to prefer a hand-made bat to the much-advertised article of their sponsors.

Leslie Ward and his son, Steve, made their 'Senior Counties' cricket bats at Ravensthorpe, near Dewsbury, for Yorkshire League teams and others in the North of England.

Bat willow (salix alba coerulea) which needs a straight grain, is cultivated in rich alluvial soil with good drainage and plenty of rain and sun. Like poplar, willow is a fast-growing tree and is usually ready for felling after 12 to 16 years' growth when it has achieved a girth nearly four feet in circumference at a height of about five feet. The best bat timber is found in the lower bole of the tree.

In bat-making, after the careful way in which the wood is sawn into 'rounds' and then into 'clefts' before being weathered, the craftsman's skill comes into its own both in the way in which the blade is shaped and rolled to obtain strength and hardness and also in achieving the right weight and balance to suit the individual player.

Leslie Ward shapes the blades and his son, Steve, looks after the handles.

Leslie Ward with the first bat he made professionally, in 1925, for Yorkshire County player Percy Holmes. Leslie's son, Steve, holds a new 'Senior Counties' bat.

Brass Band Instruments

In the twenties and thirties, all the mills in the West Riding and the collieries in South Yorkshire as well as many factories in Sheffield, Leeds and Middlesborough supported their own brass bands. As well as the few who entered the highly combative arena of the National Championship or the heady world of the National Festival, the majority provided a melodious background to the ceremonial or leisure life of Yorkshire, playing in processions, on the touch line or in parks.

In the early days of the brass band movement there were great struggles to raise money to buy instruments. Help came to these amateur musicians from a variety of sources. In the country village landlords often helped to finance local bands. Certainly this must have been a wise investment, for, inevitably, the pub became the practice room as well as the recreation room afterwards. In the Dales a number of the old leadmining companies, when times were good in the industry, sponsored bands. 'A good blow wi't'band' was regarded as good for the health of miners who spent much of their lives toiling away in dark and dank conditions underground.

Today there is still just as much of a struggle to find the money to buy new brass band instruments. Therefore very great attention is paid to keeping band instruments in fine fettle. A few firms in the North provide a skilled service for their repair.

'Shots' or cylindrical sections of steel are carefully inserted into the tubes of an instrument to allow the hammering out of dents.

Roy Wadman working on the bell of a tuba in the workshop of R S Kitchen Ltd, formerly of Queen Victoria Street, Leeds, which was founded in 1875 to repair the instruments of many of the brass bands in the North of England.